HIS Healing Power

God's Promises for Health and Wholeness

From *The King James Bible*

by Phyllis Kerley

ZOE Word

His Healing Power, God's Promises for Health and Wholeness by Phyllis Kerley

Published 2021 by ZoeWord
Louisburg, NC 27549

All Scripture quotations are from *The Holy Bible, King James Version*. 1987 printing. The KJV is public domain in the United States. Biblegateway.com

Copyright @ 2021 Phyllis Kerley

Cover and interior photos: northlightimages / iStockphoto; lavendar bundle Kotkoa / iStockphoto

All rights reserved. No part of this publication may be reproduced or transmitted in any form or by any electronic or mechanical means including photo copying, recording, or any information storage and retrieval system now known or to be invented, without permission in writing from the publisher or the author.

ISBN: 978-0-578-92312-3
Subjects: 1. RELIGION/Biblical Commentary/General
2. RELIGION/BiblicalStudies/General
3. RELIGION/Christian Ministry/Adult

Design by Robin Black, www.InspirioDesign.com

He sent his word, and healed them,
and delivered them from their destructions.
—Psalm 107:20

[20] *My son, attend to my words; incline thine ear unto my sayings.*
[21] *Let them not depart from thine eyes;*
keep them in the midst of thine heart.
[22] *For they are life unto those that find them,*
and health to all their flesh.
—Proverbs 4:20-22

INTRODUCTION

Diagnosis: CANCER.

It couldn't possibly happen to me. But it did.

From the moment the doctor told me there were evidences of suspicious calcium deposits indicated on my mammogram, and that he thought I should see a surgeon, a dark cloud seemed to descend around me. I knew what to do. I knew I should get into God's Word, but my thoughts were so scattered that I was unable to do so. I thought it couldn't possibly be anything serious enough to worry about.

The surgeon recommended that I have a biopsy. He didn't expect to find anything. We were doing this just to prove it wasn't cancer. But I couldn't shake this dark, foreboding feeling. I still couldn't concentrate enough to immerse myself in God's Word, which I knew I needed to do.

When I called to find out the results of the biopsy, the surgeon said I had "a little cancer." He said he was very surprised, and that I needed to see him the next day. He told me to bring my husband with me.

My options were a total mastectomy or a lumpectomy to be followed by radiation treatments five days a week for about seven weeks. My first reaction was to go for what I considered to be the least radical and to opt for the lumpectomy. My husband concurred, so it was scheduled for the following Wednesday morning at 7:30. We gathered up the breast cancer literature offered to us and went home, still in shock.

I started to read some of the articles on breast cancer, but suddenly, I finally realized that I needed to spend the little time left before surgery concentrating on The Healer, rather than on the disease. I got out all of the books I had collected on God's healing power and started reading them. I praised God constantly, day and night, that "by His stripes I was healed." I prayed that they would find no cancer in any of the tissue they excised or in the lymph nodes. And I just committed all the pain I was worried about unto God.

The surgery was easy. I really experienced very little pain. The nurse called me Friday afternoon with good news—there was no cancer found in the tissue excised or in the lymph nodes. No more cancer was found. Thank God. He does answer prayer.

Psalm 107:20 tells us that "He sent his word, and healed them." As I recovered from surgery, many times all I wanted to do was to immerse myself in God's Word as in a soothing whirlpool bath of healing waters. This book contains a collection of the scriptures I found on God's healing power during this experience with cancer and my recovery from it. I know the decision to concentrate my time and my energies on The Healer rather than on the disease made all the difference in my recovery. I pray that it will make a difference in your life as well, as you experience His Healing Power.

—Phyllis Kerley

OLD TESTAMENT

If thou wilt diligently hearken to the voice of the Lord thy God, and wilt do that which is right in his sight, and wilt give ear to his commandments, and keep all his statutes, I will put none of these diseases upon thee, which I have brought upon the Egyptians: for I am the Lord that healeth thee.

—Exodus 15:26

HIS HEALING POWER

¹⁷ So Abraham prayed unto God: and God healed Abimelech, and his wife, and his maidservants; and they bare children.

¹⁸ For the Lord had fast closed up all the wombs of the house of Abimelech, because of Sarah Abraham's wife.

²¹:¹ And the LORD visited Sarah as he had said, and the Lord did unto Sarah as he had spoken.

² For Sarah conceived, and bare Abraham a son in his old age, at the set time of which God had spoken to him.

—Genesis 20:17-21:2

And ye shall serve the LORD your God, and he shall bless thy bread, and thy water; and I will take sickness away from the midst of thee.

²⁶ There shall nothing cast their young, nor be barren, in thy land: the number of thy days I will fulfill.

—Exodus 23:25-26

¹⁴ Thou shalt be blessed above all people: there shall not be male or female barren among you, or among your cattle.

¹⁵ And the Lord will take away from thee all sickness, and will put none of the evil diseases of Egypt, which thou knowest, upon thee; but will lay them upon all them that hate thee.

—Deuteronomy 7:14-15

This is the Blessing of the Lord that HE promised.

The Blessing of the Lord, it maketh rich, and He addeth no sorrow with it.

—Proverbs 10:22

¹ And it shall come to pass, if thou shalt hearken diligently unto the voice of the Lord thy God, to observe and to do all his commandments which I command thee this day, that the Lord thy God will set thee on high above all nations of the earth:

² And all these blessings shall come on thee, and overtake thee, if thou shalt hearken unto the voice of the Lord thy God.

³ Blessed shalt thou be in the city, and blessed shalt thou be in the field.

⁴ Blessed shall be the fruit of thy body, and the fruit of thy ground, and the fruit of thy cattle, the increase of thy kine, and the flocks of thy sheep.

⁵ Blessed shall be thy basket and thy store.

⁶ Blessed shalt thou be when thou comest in, and blessed shalt thou be when thou goest out.

—Deuteronomy 28:1- 6

Conversely, these verses are the curse that Jesus bore on the cross for us so that we are delivered from all these things.

Christ hath redeemed us from the curse of the law, being made a curse for us: for it is written, cursed is everyone that hangeth on a tree.

—Galatians 3:13

HIS HEALING POWER

Rejoice and praise God and be glad that Christ has indeed redeemed us from all these curses and we do not have to bear them. He took them from us and paid the price on the cross as He bore them for our sakes so we can be free from every sickness and disease, even from those "not written in the book of the law".

—Deuteronomy 28:61

[15] But it shall come to pass, if thou wilt not hearken unto the voice of the Lord thy God, to observe to do all his commandments and his statutes which I command thee this day; that all these curses shall come upon thee, and overtake thee:

[16] Cursed shalt thou be in the city, and cursed shalt thou be in the field.

[17] Cursed shall be thy basket and thy store.

[18] Cursed shall be the fruit of thy body, and the fruit of thy land, the increase of thy kine, and the flocks of thy sheep.

[19] Cursed shalt thou be when thou comest in, and cursed shalt thou be when thou goest out.

[20] The Lord shall send upon thee cursing, vexation, and rebuke, in all that thou settest thine hand unto for to do, until thou be destroyed, and until thou perish quickly; because of the wickedness of thy doings, whereby thou hast forsaken me.

[21] The Lord shall make the pestilence cleave unto thee, until he have consumed thee from off the land, whither thou goest to possess it.

OLD TESTAMENT

²² The Lord shall smite thee with a consumption, and with a fever, and with an inflammation, and with an extreme burning, and with the sword, and with blasting, and with mildew; and they shall pursue thee until thou perish.

²³ And thy heaven that is over thy head shall be brass, and the earth that is under thee shall be iron.

²⁴ The Lord shall make the rain of thy land powder and dust: from heaven shall it come down upon thee, until thou be destroyed.

²⁵ The Lord shall cause thee to be smitten before thine enemies: thou shalt go out one way against them, and flee seven ways before them: and shalt be removed into all the kingdoms of the earth.

²⁶ And thy carcase shall be meat unto all fowls of the air, and unto the beasts of the earth, and no man shall fray them away.

²⁷ The Lord will smite thee with the botch of Egypt, and with the emerods, and with the scab, and with the itch, whereof thou canst not be healed.

²⁸ The Lord shall smite thee with madness, and blindness, and astonishment of heart:

²⁹ And thou shalt grope at noonday, as the blind gropeth in darkness, and thou shalt not prosper in thy ways: and thou shalt be only oppressed and spoiled evermore, and no man shall save thee.

—Deuteronomy 28:15-29

³⁵ The Lord shall smite thee in the knees, and in the legs, with a sore botch that cannot be healed, from the sole of thy foot unto the top of thy head.

⁵⁸ If thou wilt not observe to do all the words of this law that are written in this book, that thou mayest fear this glorious and fearful name, THE LORD THY GOD;

⁵⁹ Then the LORD will make thy plagues wonderful, and the plagues of thy seed, even great plagues, and of long continuance, and sore sicknesses, and of long continuance.

⁶⁰ Moreover he will bring upon thee all the diseases of Egypt, which thou wast afraid of; and they shall cleave unto thee.

⁶¹ Also every sickness, and every plague, which is not written in the book of this law, them will the LORD bring upon thee, until thou be destroyed.

—Deuteronomy 28:35, 58-61

⁶⁴ And the LORD shall scatter thee among all people, from the one end of the earth even unto the other; and there thou shalt serve other gods, which neither thou nor thy fathers have known, even wood and stone.

⁶⁵ And among these nations shalt thou find no ease, neither shall the sole of thy foot have rest: but the LORD shall give thee there a trembling heart, and failing of eyes, and sorrow of mind:

⁶⁶ And thy life shall hang in doubt before thee; and thou shalt fear day and night, and shalt have none assurance of thy life:

⁶⁷ In the morning thou shalt say, Would God it were even! and at even thou shalt say, Would God it were morning! for the fear of thine heart wherewith thou shalt fear, and for the sight of thine eyes which thou shalt see.

—Deuteronomy 28:64-67

¹³ Christ hath redeemed us from the curse of the law, being made a curse for us: for it is written, Cursed is every one that hangeth on a tree:

¹⁴ That the blessing of Abraham might come on the Gentiles through Jesus Christ; that we might receive the promise of the Spirit through faith.

²⁹ And if ye be Christ's, then are ye Abraham's seed, and heirs according to the promise.

—Galatians 3:13-14, 29

² For the law of the Spirit of life in Christ Jesus hath made me free from the law of sin and death.

¹¹ But if the Spirit of him that raised up Jesus from the dead dwell in you, he that raised up Christ from the dead shall also quicken your mortal bodies by his Spirit that dwelleth in you.

—Romans 8:2,11

⁷ Know ye therefore that they which are of faith, the same are the children of Abraham.

—Galatians 3:7

¹⁹ I call heaven and earth to record this day against you, that I have set before you life and death, blessing and cursing: therefore choose life, that both thou and thy seed may live:

²⁰ That thou mayest love the Lord thy God, and that thou mayest obey his voice, and that thou mayest cleave unto him: for he is thy life, and the length of thy days: that thou mayest dwell in the land which the Lord sware unto thy fathers, to Abraham, to Isaac, and to Jacob, to give them.

—Deuteronomy 30:19-20

This book of the law shall not depart out of thy mouth; but thou shalt meditate therein day and night, that thou mayest observe to do according to all that is written therein: for then thou shalt make thy way prosperous, and then thou shalt have good success.

—Joshua 1:8

There failed not ought of any good thing which the Lord had spoken unto the house of Israel; all came to pass.

—Joshua 21:45

Blessed be the Lord, that hath given rest unto his people Israel, according to all that he promised: there hath not failed one word of all his good promise, which he promised by the hand of Moses his servant.

—1 Kings 8:56

And Jabez called on the God of Israel, saying, Oh that thou wouldest bless me indeed, and enlarge my coast, and that thine hand might be with me, and that thou wouldest keep me from evil, that it may not grieve me! And God granted him that which he requested.

—1 Chronicles 4:10

For the eyes of the Lord run to and fro throughout the whole earth, to shew himself strong in the behalf of them whose heart is perfect toward him. Herein thou hast done foolishly: therefore from henceforth thou shalt have wars.

—2 Chronicles 16:9

¹⁸ For a multitude of the people, even many of Ephraim, and Manasseh, Issachar, and Zebulun, had not cleansed themselves, yet did they eat the passover otherwise than it was written. But Hezekiah prayed for them, saying, The good LORD pardon every one

¹⁹ That prepareth his heart to seek God, the LORD God of his fathers, though he be not cleansed according to the purification of the sanctuary.

²⁰ And the LORD hearkened to Hezekiah, and healed the people.

—2 Chronicles 30:18-20

Then he said unto them, Go your way, eat the fat, and drink the sweet, and send portions unto them for whom nothing is prepared: for this day is holy unto our LORD: neither be ye sorry; for the joy of the LORD is your strength.

—Nehemiah 8:10

± Sing praises to the LORD, which dwelleth in Zion: declare among the people his doings.

¹² When he maketh inquisition for blood, he remembereth them: he forgetteth not the cry of the humble.

—Psalm 9:11-12

¹ The Lord is my shepherd; I shall not want.

² He maketh me to lie down in green pastures: he leadeth me beside the still waters.

³ He restoreth my soul: he leadeth me in the paths of righteousness for his name's sake.

⁴ Yea, though I walk through the valley of the shadow of death, I will fear no evil: for thou art with me; thy rod and thy staff they comfort me.

⁵ Thou preparest a table before me in the presence of mine enemies: thou anointest my head with oil; my cup runneth over.

⁶ Surely goodness and mercy shall follow me all the days of my life: and I will dwell in the house of the Lord for ever.

—Psalm 23

Mine eyes are ever toward the Lord; for he shall pluck my feet out of the net.

—Psalm 25:15

The Lord is my light and my salvation; whom shall I fear? the Lord is the strength of my life; of whom shall I be afraid?

—Psalm 27:1

⁶ Blessed be the Lord, because he hath heard the voice of my supplications.

⁷ The Lord is my strength and my shield; my heart trusted in him, and I am helped: therefore my heart greatly rejoiceth; and with my song will I praise him.

⁸ The Lord is their strength, and he is the saving strength of his anointed.

—Psalm 28:6-8

The Lord will give strength unto his people; the Lord will bless his people with peace.

—Psalm 29:11

² O Lord my God, I cried unto thee, and thou hast healed me.

³ O Lord, thou hast brought up my soul from the grave: thou hast kept me alive, that I should not go down to the pit.

⁴ Sing unto the Lord, O ye saints of his, and give thanks at the remembrance of his holiness.

⁵ For his anger endureth but a moment; in his favour is life: weeping may endure for a night, but joy cometh in the morning.

—Psalm 30:2-5

Thou art my hiding place; thou shalt preserve me from trouble; thou shalt compass me about with songs of deliverance. Selah.

—Psalm 32:7

¹ I will bless the Lord at all times: his praise shall continually be in my mouth.

² My soul shall make her boast in the Lord: the humble shall hear thereof, and be glad.

³ O magnify the Lord with me, and let us exalt his name together.

⁴ I sought the Lord, and he heard me, and delivered me from all my fears.

⁵ They looked unto him, and were lightened: and their faces were not ashamed.

⁶ This poor man cried, and the Lord heard him, and saved him out of all his troubles.

⁷ The angel of the Lord encampeth round about them that fear him, and delivereth them.

⁸ O taste and see that the Lord is good: blessed is the man that trusteth in him.

⁹ O fear the Lord, ye his saints: for there is no want to them that fear him.

¹⁰ The young lions do lack, and suffer hunger: but they that seek the Lord shall not want any good thing.

HIS HEALING POWER

¹¹ Come, ye children, hearken unto me: I will teach you the fear of the Lord.

¹² What man is he that desireth life, and loveth many days, that he may see good?

¹³ Keep thy tongue from evil, and thy lips from speaking guile.

¹⁴ Depart from evil, and do good; seek peace, and pursue it.

¹⁵ The eyes of the Lord are upon the righteous, and his ears are open unto their cry.

¹⁶ The face of the Lord is against them that do evil, to cut off the remembrance of them from the earth.

¹⁷ The righteous cry, and the Lord heareth, and delivereth them out of all their troubles.

¹⁸ The Lord is nigh unto them that are of a broken heart; and saveth such as be of a contrite spirit.

¹⁹ Many are the afflictions of the righteous: but the Lord delivereth him out of them all.

²⁰ He keepeth all his bones: not one of them is broken.

²¹ Evil shall slay the wicked: and they that hate the righteous shall be desolate.

22 The Lord redeemeth the soul of his servants: and none of them that trust in him shall be desolate.

—Psalm 34

²⁷ Let them shout for joy, and be glad, that favour my righteous cause: yea, let them say continually, Let the Lord be magnified, which hath pleasure in the prosperity of his servant.

²⁸ And my tongue shall speak of thy righteousness and of thy praise all the day long.

—Psalm 35:27-28

OLD TESTAMENT

³ Trust in the LORD, and do good; so shalt thou dwell in the land, and verily thou shalt be fed.

⁴ Delight thyself also in the LORD: and he shall give thee the desires of thine heart.
—Psalm 37:3-4

¹ Blessed is he that considereth the poor: the LORD will deliver him in time of trouble.

² The LORD will preserve him, and keep him alive; and he shall be blessed upon the earth: and thou wilt not deliver him unto the will of his enemies.

³ The LORD will strengthen him upon the bed of languishing: thou wilt make all his bed in his sickness.
—Psalm 41:1-3

¹⁴ Offer unto God thanksgiving; and pay thy vows unto the most High:

¹⁵ And call upon me in the day of trouble: I will deliver thee, and thou shalt glorify me.
—Psalm 50:14-15

¹⁰ Create in me a clean heart, O God; and renew a right spirit within me.

¹¹ Cast me not away from thy presence; and take not thy holy spirit from me.

¹² Restore unto me the joy of thy salvation; and uphold me with thy free spirit.
—Psalm 51:10-12

Behold, God is mine helper: the Lord is with them that uphold my soul.
—Psalm 54:4

⁶ I will freely sacrifice unto thee: I will praise thy name, O Lord; for it is good.

⁷ For he hath delivered me out of all trouble: and mine eye hath seen his desire upon mine enemies.

—Psalm 54:6-7

Cast thy burden upon the Lord, and he shall sustain thee: he shall never suffer the righteous to be moved.

—Psalm 55:22

Be merciful unto me, O God, be merciful unto me: for my soul trusteth in thee: yea, in the shadow of thy wings will I make my refuge, until these calamities be overpast.

—Psalm 57:1

¹⁶ But I will sing of thy power; yea, I will sing aloud of thy mercy in the morning: for thou hast been my defence and refuge in the day of my trouble.

¹⁷ Unto thee, O my strength, will I sing: for God is my defence, and the God of my mercy.

—Psalm 59:16-17

1 Truly my soul waiteth upon God: from him cometh my salvation.

² He only is my rock and my salvation; he is my defence; I shall not be greatly moved.

—Psalm 62:1-2

⁷ Because thou hast been my help, therefore in the shadow of thy wings will I rejoice.

⁸ My soul followeth hard after thee: thy right hand upholdeth me.

—Psalm 63:7-8

¹⁹ Blessed be the Lord, who daily loadeth us with benefits, even the God of our salvation. Selah.

²⁰ He that is our God is the God of salvation; and unto God the Lord belong the issues from death.

—Psalm 68:19-20

O God, thou art terrible out of thy holy places: the God of Israel is he that giveth strength and power unto his people. Blessed be God.

—Psalm 68:35

But I am poor and needy: make haste unto me, O God: thou art my help and my deliverer; O Lord, make no tarrying.

—Psalm 70:5

¹³ Thy way, O God, is in the sanctuary: who is so great a God as our God?

¹⁴ Thou art the God that doest wonders: thou hast declared thy strength among the people.

—Psalm 77:13-14

Turn us again, O God, and cause thy face to shine; and we shall be saved.

—Psalm 80:3

¹ He that dwelleth in the secret place of the most High shall abide under the shadow of the Almighty.

² I will say of the Lord, He is my refuge and my fortress: my God; in him will I trust.

³ Surely he shall deliver thee from the snare of the fowler, and from the noisome pestilence.

HIS HEALING POWER

⁴ He shall cover thee with his feathers, and under his wings shalt thou trust: his truth shall be thy shield and buckler.

⁵ Thou shalt not be afraid for the terror by night; nor for the arrow that flieth by day;

⁶ Nor for the pestilence that walketh in darkness; nor for the destruction that wasteth at noonday.

⁷ A thousand shall fall at thy side, and ten thousand at thy right hand; but it shall not come nigh thee.

⁸ Only with thine eyes shalt thou behold and see the reward of the wicked.

⁹ Because thou hast made the LORD, which is my refuge, even the most High, thy habitation;

¹⁰ There shall no evil befall thee, neither shall any plague come nigh thy dwelling.

¹¹ For he shall give his angels charge over thee, to keep thee in all thy ways.

¹² They shall bear thee up in their hands, lest thou dash thy foot against a stone.

¹³ Thou shalt tread upon the lion and adder: the young lion and the dragon shalt thou trample under feet.

¹⁴ Because he hath set his love upon me, therefore will I deliver him: I will set him on high, because he hath known my name.

¹⁵ He shall call upon me, and I will answer him: I will be with him in trouble; I will deliver him, and honour him.

¹⁶ With long life will I satisfy him, and shew him my salvation.

—Psalm 91

¹² The righteous shall flourish like the palm tree: he shall grow like a cedar in Lebanon.

¹³ Those that be planted in the house of the LORD shall flourish in the courts of our God.

¹⁴ They shall still bring forth fruit in old age; they shall be fat and flourishing;

¹⁵ To shew that the LORD is upright: he is my rock, and there is no unrighteousness in him.

—Psalm 92:12-15

¹⁸ When I said, My foot slippeth; thy mercy, O Lord, held me up.

¹⁹ In the multitude of my thoughts within me thy comforts delight my soul.

—Psalm 94:18-19

¹ Bless the LORD, O my soul: and all that is within me, bless his holy name.

² Bless the LORD, O my soul, and forget not all his benefits:

³ Who forgiveth all thine iniquities; who healeth all thy diseases;

⁴ Who redeemeth thy life from destruction; who crowneth thee with lovingkindness and tender mercies;

⁵ Who satisfieth thy mouth with good things; so that thy youth is renewed like the eagle's.

—Psalm 103:1-5

He brought them forth also with silver and gold: and there was not one feeble person among their tribes.

—Psalm 105:37

[19] Then they cry unto the LORD in their trouble, and he saveth them out of their distresses.

[20] He sent his word, and healed them, and delivered them from their destructions.

[21] Oh that men would praise the LORD for his goodness, and for his wonderful works to the children of men!

[22] And let them sacrifice the sacrifices of thanksgiving, and declare his works with rejoicing.

—Psalm 107:19-22

[1] I love the LORD, because he hath heard my voice and my supplications.

[2] Because he hath inclined his ear unto me, therefore will I call upon him as long as I live.

[3] The sorrows of death compassed me, and the pains of hell gat hold upon me: I found trouble and sorrow.

[4] Then called I upon the name of the LORD; O LORD, I beseech thee, deliver my soul.

[5] Gracious is the LORD, and righteous; yea, our God is merciful.

[6] The LORD preserveth the simple: I was brought low, and he helped me.

[7] Return unto thy rest, O my soul; for the LORD hath dealt bountifully with thee.

[8] For thou hast delivered my soul from death, mine eyes from tears, and my feet from falling.

[9] I will walk before the LORD in the land of the living.

—Psalm 116:1-9

I shall not die, but live, and declare the works of the LORD.

—Psalm 118:17

This is my comfort in my affliction: for thy word hath quickened me.

—Psalm 119:50

⁷⁶ Let, I pray thee, thy merciful kindness be for my comfort, according to thy word unto thy servant.

⁷⁷ Let thy tender mercies come unto me, that I may live: for thy law is my delight.

—Psalm 119:76-77

¹ I will lift up mine eyes unto the hills, from whence cometh my help.

² My help cometh from the Lord, which made heaven and earth.

³ He will not suffer thy foot to be moved: he that keepeth thee will not slumber.

⁴ Behold, he that keepeth Israel shall neither slumber nor sleep.

⁵ The Lord is thy keeper: the Lord is thy shade upon thy right hand.

⁶ The sun shall not smite thee by day, nor the moon by night.

⁷ The Lord shall preserve thee from all evil: he shall preserve thy soul.

⁸ The Lord shall preserve thy going out and thy coming in from this time forth, and even for evermore.

—Psalm 121

⁷ Though I walk in the midst of trouble, thou wilt revive me: thou shalt stretch forth thine hand against the wrath of mine enemies, and thy right hand shall save me.

⁸ The Lord will perfect that which concerneth me: thy mercy, O Lord, endureth for ever: forsake not the works of thine own hands.

—Psalm 138:7-8

Quicken me, O Lord, for thy name's sake: for thy righteousness' sake bring my soul out of trouble.

—Psalm 143:11

⁸ The Lord is gracious, and full of compassion; slow to anger, and of great mercy.

⁹ The Lord is good to all: and his tender mercies are over all his works.

—Psalm 145:8-9

¹³ Thy kingdom is an everlasting kingdom, and thy dominion endureth throughout all generations.

¹⁴ The Lord upholdeth all that fall, and raiseth up all those that be bowed down.

¹⁵ The eyes of all wait upon thee; and thou givest them their meat in due season.

¹⁶ Thou openest thine hand, and satisfiest the desire of every living thing.

¹⁷ The Lord is righteous in all his ways, and holy in all his works.

¹⁸ The Lord is nigh unto all them that call upon him, to all that call upon him in truth.

¹⁹ He will fulfil the desire of them that fear him: he also will hear their cry, and will save them.

²⁰ The Lord preserveth all them that love him: but all the wicked will he destroy.

[21] My mouth shall speak the praise of the Lord: and let all flesh bless his holy name for ever and ever.
—Psalm 145:13-21

The Lord openeth the eyes of the blind: the Lord raiseth them that are bowed down: the Lord loveth the righteous:
—Psalm 146:8

He healeth the broken in heart, and bindeth up their wounds.
—Psalm 147:3

The fear of the Lord is the beginning of knowledge: but fools despise wisdom and instruction.
—Proverbs 1:7

But whoso hearkeneth unto me shall dwell safely, and shall be quiet from fear of evil.
—Proverbs 1:33

[1] My son, forget not my law; but let thine heart keep my commandments:

[2] For length of days, and long life, and peace, shall they add to thee.

[3] Let not mercy and truth forsake thee: bind them about thy neck; write them upon the table of thine heart:

[4] So shalt thou find favour and good understanding in the sight of God and man.

[5] Trust in the Lord with all thine heart; and lean not unto thine own understanding.

[6] In all thy ways acknowledge him, and he shall direct thy paths.

⁷ Be not wise in thine own eyes: fear the LORD, and depart from evil.

⁸ It shall be health to thy navel, and marrow to thy bones.

—Proverbs 3:1-8

God promises us health, long life, and peace as we trust in Him and keep His commandments.

¹³ Happy is the man that findeth wisdom, and the man that getteth understanding.

¹⁴ For the merchandise of it is better than the merchandise of silver, and the gain thereof than fine gold.

¹⁵ She is more precious than rubies: and all the things thou canst desire are not to be compared unto her.

¹⁶ Length of days is in her right hand; and in her left hand riches and honour.

¹⁷ Her ways are ways of pleasantness, and all her paths are peace.

¹⁸ She is a tree of life to them that lay hold upon her: and happy is every one that retaineth her.

—Proverbs 3:13-18

²¹ My son, let not them depart from thine eyes: keep sound wisdom and discretion:

²² So shall they be life unto thy soul, and grace to thy neck.

²³ Then shalt thou walk in thy way safely, and thy foot shall not stumble.

²⁴ When thou liest down, thou shalt not be afraid: yea, thou shalt lie down, and thy sleep shall be sweet.

²⁵ Be not afraid of sudden fear, neither of the desolation of the wicked, when it cometh.

²⁶ For the Lord shall be thy confidence, and shall keep thy foot from being taken.
—Proverbs 3:21-26

God's WORD is our Life! When we spend time meditating on God's WORD, it is health and strength to our flesh, as well as to our spirits!

²⁰ My son, attend to my words; incline thine ear unto my sayings.

²¹ Let them not depart from thine eyes; keep them in the midst of thine heart.

²² For they are life unto those that find them, and health to all their flesh.

²³ Keep thy heart with all diligence; for out of it are the issues of life.

²⁴ Put away from thee a froward mouth, and perverse lips put far from thee.

²⁵ Let thine eyes look right on, and let thine eyelids look straight before thee.

²⁶ Ponder the path of thy feet, and let all thy ways be established.

²⁷ Turn not to the right hand nor to the left: remove thy foot from evil.
—Proverbs 4:20-27

The mouth of a righteous man is a well of life: but violence covereth the mouth of the wicked.
—Proverbs 10:11

There is that speaketh like the piercings of a sword: but the tongue of the wise is health.
—Proverbs 12:18

He that keepeth his mouth keepeth his life: but he that openeth wide his lips shall have destruction.

—Proverbs 13:3

A sound heart is the life of the flesh: but envy the rottenness of the bones.

—Proverbs 14:30

A wholesome tongue is a tree of life: but perverseness therein is a breach in the spirit.

—Proverbs 15:4

The light of the eyes rejoiceth the heart: and a good report maketh the bones fat.

—Proverbs 15:30

Understanding is a wellspring of life unto him that hath it: but the instruction of fools is folly.

—Proverbs 16:22

Pleasant words are as an honeycomb, sweet to the soul, and health to the bones.

—Proverbs 16:24

A merry heart doeth good like a medicine: but a broken spirit drieth the bones.

—Proverbs 17:22

Death and life are in the power of the tongue: and they that love it shall eat the fruit thereof.

—Proverbs 18:21

By humility and the fear of the Lord are riches, and honour, and life.

—Proverbs 22:4

And the head of Ephraim is Samaria, and the head of Samaria is Remaliah's son. If ye will not believe, surely ye shall not be established.

—Isaiah 7:9

You will keep in perfect peace him whose mind is steadfast, because he trusts in you.

— Isaiah 26:3

¹ In those days was Hezekiah sick unto death. And Isaiah the prophet the son of Amoz came unto him, and said unto him, Thus saith the Lord, Set thine house in order: for thou shalt die, and not live.

² Then Hezekiah turned his face toward the wall, and prayed unto the Lord,

³ And said, Remember now, O Lord, I beseech thee, how I have walked before thee in truth and with a perfect heart, and have done that which is good in thy sight. And Hezekiah wept sore.

⁴ Then came the word of the Lord to Isaiah, saying,

⁵ Go, and say to Hezekiah, Thus saith the Lord, the God of David thy father, I have heard thy prayer, I have seen thy tears: behold, I will add unto thy days fifteen years.

⁶ And I will deliver thee and this city out of the hand of the king of Assyria: and I will defend this city.

⁷ And this shall be a sign unto thee from the Lord, that the Lord will do this thing that he hath spoken;

⁸ Behold, I will bring again the shadow of the degrees, which is gone down in the sun dial of Ahaz, ten degrees backward. So the sun returned ten degrees, by which degrees it was gone down.

—Isaiah 38:1-8

[15] What shall I say? he hath both spoken unto me, and himself hath done it: I shall go softly all my years in the bitterness of my soul.

[16] O Lord, by these things men live, and in all these things is the life of my spirit: so wilt thou recover me, and make me to live.

— Isaiah 38:15-16

[28] Hast thou not known? hast thou not heard, that the everlasting God, the Lord, the Creator of the ends of the earth, fainteth not, neither is weary? there is no searching of his understanding.

[29] He giveth power to the faint; and to them that have no might he increaseth strength.

[30] Even the youths shall faint and be weary, and the young men shall utterly fall:

[31] But they that wait upon the Lord shall renew their strength; they shall mount up with wings as eagles; they shall run, and not be weary; and they shall walk, and not faint.

—Isaiah 40:28-31

Fear thou not; for I am with thee: be not dismayed; for I am thy God: I will strengthen thee; yea, I will help thee; yea, I will uphold thee with the right hand of my righteousness.

—Isaiah 41:10

[4] Surely he hath borne our griefs, and carried our sorrows: yet we did esteem him stricken, smitten of God, and afflicted.

⁵ But he was wounded for our transgressions, he was bruised for our iniquities: the chastisement of our peace was upon him; and with his stripes we are healed.

—Isaiah 53:4-5

The Prophet Isaiah looked ahead in time to see Jesus our Lord hanging on the cross. Broken and bleeding, He willingly took all our sins on Himself and bore them and died, so we can be forgiven of them and have eternal life in Him. He also bore our griefs and sorrows (or sicknesses and diseases) so we don't have to bear them. He took them upon Himself and gave us healing. He became our scapegoat. Our sins, sicknesses, and diseases are gone forever when we believe on Him and commit them to Him. For with His stripes we ARE healed! Praise God!!!

⁶ For the LORD hath called thee as a woman forsaken and grieved in spirit, and a wife of youth, when thou wast refused, saith thy God.

⁷ For a small moment have I forsaken thee; but with great mercies will I gather thee.

⁸ In a little wrath I hid my face from thee for a moment; but with everlasting kindness will I have mercy on thee, saith the LORD thy Redeemer.

⁹ For this is as the waters of Noah unto me: for as I have sworn that the waters of Noah should no more go over the earth; so have I sworn that I would not be wroth with thee, nor rebuke thee.

¹⁰ For the mountains shall depart, and the hills be removed; but my kindness shall not depart from thee, neither shall the covenant of my peace be removed, saith the Lord that hath mercy on thee.

¹¹ O thou afflicted, tossed with tempest, and not comforted, behold, I will lay thy stones with fair colours, and lay thy foundations with sapphires.

¹² And I will make thy windows of agates, and thy gates of carbuncles, and all thy borders of pleasant stones.

¹³ And all thy children shall be taught of the Lord; and great shall be the peace of thy children.

¹⁴ In righteousness shalt thou be established: thou shalt be far from oppression; for thou shalt not fear: and from terror; for it shall not come near thee.

¹⁵ Behold, they shall surely gather together, but not by me: whosoever shall gather together against thee shall fall for thy sake.

¹⁶ Behold, I have created the smith that bloweth the coals in the fire, and that bringeth forth an instrument for his work; and I have created the waster to destroy.

¹⁷ No weapon that is formed against thee shall prosper; and every tongue that shall rise against thee in judgment thou shalt condemn. This is the heritage of the servants of the Lord, and their righteousness is of me, saith the Lord.

—Isaiah 54:6-17

Verse 17 says "no weapon formed against thee shall prosper." That includes all sicknesses and diseases. Jesus told us that the enemy comes to kill, steal, and destroy. Sicknesses and diseases

are from the enemy. (John 10:10) Verse 17 tells us that these weapons of the enemy shall not prosper against the servants of the Lord. Jesus bought and paid for our healing on the cross. Healing is the heritage of the servants of the Lord.

⁶ Seek ye the Lord while he may be found, call ye upon him while he is near:

⁷ Let the wicked forsake his way, and the unrighteous man his thoughts: and let him return unto the Lord, and he will have mercy upon him; and to our God, for he will abundantly pardon.

⁸ For my thoughts are not your thoughts, neither are your ways my ways, saith the Lord.

⁹ For as the heavens are higher than the earth, so are my ways higher than your ways, and my thoughts than your thoughts.

¹⁰ For as the rain cometh down, and the snow from heaven, and returneth not thither, but watereth the earth, and maketh it bring forth and bud, that it may give seed to the sower, and bread to the eater:

¹¹ So shall my word be that goeth forth out of my mouth: it shall not return unto me void, but it shall accomplish that which I please, and it shall prosper in the thing whereto I sent it.

¹² For ye shall go out with joy, and be led forth with peace: the mountains and the hills shall break forth before you into singing, and all the trees of the field shall clap their hands.

¹³ Instead of the thorn shall come up the fir tree, and instead of the brier shall come up the myrtle tree: and it

shall be to the LORD for a name, for an everlasting sign that shall not be cut off.

—Isaiah 55:6-13

Even if you have turned away from God, return to Him. He will abundantly pardon you if you ask for His forgiveness. He casts all of our sins into the Sea of Forgetfulness, never to be remembered again. He welcomes you back into His family and restores to you the heritage Jesus purchased for those who believe in Him. He sent His WORD and it healed them.

[18] I have seen his ways, and will heal him: I will lead him also, and restore comforts unto him and to his mourners.

[19] I create the fruit of the lips; Peace, peace to him that is far off, and to him that is near, saith the LORD; and I will heal him.

—Isaiah 57:18-19

[6] Is not this the fast that I have chosen? To loose the bands of wickedness, to undo the heavy burdens, and to let the oppressed go free, and that ye break every yoke?

[7] Is it not to deal thy bread to the hungry, and that thou bring the poor that are cast out to thy house? when thou seest the naked, that thou cover him; and that thou hide not thyself from thine own flesh?

[8] Then shall thy light break forth as the morning, and thine health shall spring forth speedily: and thy righteousness shall go before thee; the glory of the LORD shall be thy reward.

[9] Then shalt thou call, and the LORD shall answer; thou shalt cry, and he shall say, Here I am. If thou take

away from the midst of thee the yoke, the putting forth of the finger, and speaking vanity;

¹⁰ And if thou draw out thy soul to the hungry, and satisfy the afflicted soul; then shall thy light rise in obscurity, and thy darkness be as the noon day:

¹¹ And the LORD shall guide thee continually, and satisfy thy soul in drought, and make fat thy bones: and thou shalt be like a watered garden, and like a spring of water, whose waters fail not.

—Isaiah 58:6-11

Then said the LORD unto me, Thou hast well seen: for I will hasten my word to perform it.

—Jeremiah 1:12

Heal me, O LORD, and I shall be healed; save me, and I shall be saved: for thou art my praise.

—Jeremiah 17:14

For I will restore health unto thee, and I will heal thee of thy wounds, saith the LORD; because they called thee an Outcast, saying, this is Zion, whom no man seeketh after.

—Jeremiah 30:17

Call unto me, and I will answer thee, and show thee great and mighty things, which thou knowest not.

—Jeremiah 33:3

Behold, I will bring it health and cure, and I will cure them, and will reveal unto them the abundance of peace and truth.

—Jeremiah 33:6

²¹ This I recall to my mind, therefore have I hope.

²² It is of the Lord's mercies that we are not consumed, because his compassions fail not.

²³ They are new every morning: great is thy faithfulness.

²⁴ The Lord is my portion, saith my soul; therefore will I hope in him.

²⁵ The Lord is good unto them that wait for him, to the soul that seeketh him.

²⁶ It is good that a man should both hope and quietly wait for the salvation of the Lord.

—Lamentations 3:21-26

Beat your plowshares into swords and your pruning hooks into spears: let the weak say, I am strong.

—Joel 3:10

But if ye turn unto me, and keep my commandments, and do them; though there were of you cast out unto the uttermost part of the heaven, yet will I gather them from thence, and will bring them unto the place that I have chosen to set my name there.

—Nehemiah. 1:9

² But unto you that fear my name shall the Sun of righteousness arise with healing in his wings; and ye shall go forth, and grow up as calves of the stall.

³ And ye shall tread down the wicked; for they shall be ashes under the soles of your feet in the day that I shall do this, saith the Lord of hosts.

—Malachi 4:2-3

Malachi 4:2 is the verse I visualized and repeated over and over to myself as I was lying in the machine with radiation pouring over the cancer in my body. I saw Jesus in the sky above me in all His Glory, with bright healing rays emanating from all around Him. Those rays of healing penetrated my body and healed me of that cancer. It was a very peaceful and blessed experience to meet my Healer every day and worship Him as I underwent radiation treatments. It is by His stripes indeed that I am the healed and the redeemed! Praise God!!!

NEW TESTAMENT

How God anointed Jesus of Nazareth with the Holy Ghost and with power: who went about doing good, and healing all that were oppressed of the devil; for God was with Him.
—Acts 10:38

...and He healed them all.
—Matthew 12:15

HIS HEALING POWER

The four gospels tell us about Jesus' healing ministry. He taught and preached God's WORD that was available in that day—The Torah and the Prophets. He found Himself in those writings as He studied them. He told us that He only did what God the Father told Him to do and only said what God the Father told Him to say. He went about teaching and preaching and doing good and healing ALL who were oppressed of the devil. (Acts 10:38) Yes. The devil is the author of sickness and disease. He comes to steal, kill, and destroy. Jesus came that we may have life. And have it more abundantly.

It is not recorded anywhere that He said "no" to anyone who asked Him for healing. The Canaanite woman who asked Jesus to heal her daughter was told healing was for the children of Israel first. When she gave Him an answer in faith, He healed her daughter. (Mt. 15:21-28)

He told her she had great faith so He granted her request. That is His prerequisite for granting our requests for our healing or any other blessing. He often said to the people He healed, "Your faith has made you whole." Or "Be it unto you as you have believed."

He asked the blind man Bartimaeus what he would have Him do for him. When he received his sight, Jesus told him his faith had healed him. (Mk. 10:51-52) Not Jesus' faith. It was Bartimaeus' faith that healed him.

NEW TESTAMENT

It takes faith to please God. "So then faith cometh by hearing, and hearing by the **WORD** of God." (Rom. 10:17) That is the first prerequisite necessary to receive our healing. We must first believe that God is who He says He is. The first promise He made to His people when He brought them out of Egypt is: "For I AM the Lord that healeth thee." (Ex. 15:26)

We must also believe that God can heal us, and most importantly that God will heal us. Why? How can we be so sure of that? Because God said in His **WORD** that He is the Healer. Jesus said He is like His Father. He said and did what His Father said and did. If we know Him we know the Father.

Jesus spent His life walking around, healing and blessing **ALL**. He told us that if we asked God for **ANYTHING** in His **NAME** God would do it for us. He also said in John 17:17 that God's **WORD** is truth. In John 8:31-32 Jesus said that we can know the truth and the truth will make us free. And how do we know the truth? Read and study and meditate on His **WORD**. It is The Truth. There are not many truths, as some teach today. Jesus said God's **WORD** is The Truth that will make you free. Free from what? Sickness and disease. Griefs and sorrows. All that is contained in the curse in Deuteronomy 28:15-68. Jesus delivered us from it all on the cross. Jesus is the truth. (Jn. 1:1-14) As we read and meditate on God's **WORD**, we are made free from whatever binds us. The Anointing—Jesus the Christ or the Messiah—the WORD that became flesh and made His dwelling among us—makes us free. The Anointing destroys the yoke of bondage. Not breaks it so that it can be fixed and put back together. Destroys. Dissolves. As rust dissolves iron. Jesus destroys the satanic yoke of bondage and makes us free indeed. Healed and set free from sickness and disease. (Is. 10:27, Lu. 17:11-19)

^{23} And Jesus went about all Galilee, teaching in their synagogues, and preaching the gospel of the kingdom, and healing all manner of sickness and all manner of disease among the people.

^{24} And his fame went throughout all Syria: and they brought unto him all sick people that were taken with divers diseases and torments, and those which were possessed with devils, and those which were lunatick, and those that had the palsy; and he healed them.

—Matthew 4:23-24

^{25} Therefore I say unto you, Take no thought for your life, what ye shall eat, or what ye shall drink; nor yet for your body, what ye shall put on. Is not the life more than meat, and the body than raiment?

^{26} Behold the fowls of the air: for they sow not, neither do they reap, nor gather into barns; yet your heavenly Father feedeth them. Are ye not much better than they?

^{27} Which of you by taking thought can add one cubit unto his stature?

³³ But seek ye first the kingdom of God, and his righteousness; and all these things shall be added unto you.

³⁴ Take therefore no thought for the morrow: for the morrow shall take thought for the things of itself. Sufficient unto the day is the evil thereof.

—Matthew 6:25-27, 33-34

² And, behold, there came a leper and worshipped him, saying, Lord, if thou wilt, thou canst make me clean.

³ And Jesus put forth his hand, and touched him, saying, I will; be thou clean. And immediately his leprosy was cleansed.

—Matthew 8:2-3

⁵ And when Jesus was entered into Capernaum, there came unto him a centurion, beseeching him,

⁶ And saying, Lord, my servant lieth at home sick of the palsy, grievously tormented.

⁷ And Jesus saith unto him, I will come and heal him.

⁸ The centurion answered and said, Lord, I am not worthy that thou shouldest come under my roof: but speak the word only, and my servant shall be healed.

⁹ For I am a man under authority, having soldiers under me: and I say to this man, Go, and he goeth; and to another, Come, and he cometh; and to my servant, Do this, and he doeth it.

¹⁰ When Jesus heard it, he marvelled, and said to them that followed, Verily I say unto you, I have not found so great faith, no, not in Israel.

¹¹ And I say unto you, That many shall come from the east and west, and shall sit down with Abraham, and Isaac, and Jacob, in the kingdom of heaven.

[12] But the children of the kingdom shall be cast out into outer darkness: there shall be weeping and gnashing of teeth.

[13] And Jesus said unto the centurion, Go thy way; and as thou hast believed, so be it done unto thee. And his servant was healed in the selfsame hour.

—Matthew 8:5-13

[14] And when Jesus was come into Peter's house, he saw his wife's mother laid, and sick of a fever.

[15] And he touched her hand, and the fever left her: and she arose, and ministered unto them.

—Matthew 8:14-15

[18] While he spake these things unto them, behold, there came a certain ruler, and worshipped him, saying, My daughter is even now dead: but come and lay thy hand upon her, and she shall live.

[19] And Jesus arose, and followed him, and so did his disciples.

[20] And, behold, a woman, which was diseased with an issue of blood twelve years, came behind him, and touched the hem of his garment:

[21] For she said within herself, If I may but touch his garment, I shall be whole.

[22] But Jesus turned him about, and when he saw her, he said, Daughter, be of good comfort; thy faith hath made thee whole. And the woman was made whole from that hour.

[23] And when Jesus came into the ruler's house, and saw the minstrels and the people making a noise,

[24] He said unto them, Give place: for the maid is not dead, but sleepeth. And they laughed him to scorn.

[25] But when the people were put forth, he went in, and took her by the hand, and the maid arose.

[26] And the fame hereof went abroad into all that land.

[27] And when Jesus departed thence, two blind men followed him, crying, and saying, Thou son of David, have mercy on us.

[28] And when he was come into the house, the blind men came to him: and Jesus saith unto them, Believe ye that I am able to do this? They said unto him, Yea, Lord.

29 Then touched he their eyes, saying, According to your faith be it unto you.

30 And their eyes were opened; and Jesus straitly charged them, saying, See that no man know it.

—Matthew 9:18-30

[35] And Jesus went about all the cities and villages, teaching in their synagogues, and preaching the gospel of the kingdom, and healing every sickness and every disease among the people.

[36] But when he saw the multitudes, he was moved with compassion on them, because they fainted, and were scattered abroad, as sheep having no shepherd.

—Matthew 9:35-36

[1] And when he had called unto him his twelve disciples, he gave them power against unclean spirits, to cast them out, and to heal all manner of sickness and all manner of disease.

⁵ These twelve Jesus sent forth, and commanded them, saying, Go not into the way of the Gentiles, and into any city of the Samaritans enter ye not:

⁶ But go rather to the lost sheep of the house of Israel.

⁷ And as ye go, preach, saying, The kingdom of heaven is at hand.

⁸ Heal the sick, cleanse the lepers, raise the dead, cast out devils: freely ye have received, freely give.

—Matthew 10:1, 5-8

⁹ And when he was departed thence, he went into their synagogue:

¹⁰ And, behold, there was a man which had his hand withered. And they asked him, saying, Is it lawful to heal on the sabbath days? that they might accuse him.

¹¹ And he said unto them, What man shall there be among you, that shall have one sheep, and if it fall into a pit on the sabbath day, will he not lay hold on it, and lift it out?

¹² How much then is a man better than a sheep? Wherefore it is lawful to do well on the sabbath days.

¹³ Then saith he to the man, Stretch forth thine hand. And he stretched it forth; and it was restored whole, like as the other.

¹⁴ Then the Pharisees went out, and held a council against him, how they might destroy him.

¹⁵ But when Jesus knew it, he withdrew himself from thence: and great multitudes followed him, and he healed them all.

—Matthew 12:9-15

Then was brought unto him one possessed with a devil, blind, and dumb: and he healed him, insomuch that the blind and dumb both spake and saw.

—Matthew 12:22

And Jesus went forth, and saw a great multitude, and was moved with compassion toward them, and he healed their sick.

—Matthew 14:14

34 And when they were gone over, they came into the land of Gennesaret.

35 And when the men of that place had knowledge of him, they sent out into all that country round about, and brought unto him all that were diseased;

36 And besought him that they might only touch the hem of his garment: and as many as touched were made perfectly whole.

—Matthew 14:34-36

30 And great multitudes came unto him, having with them those that were lame, blind, dumb, maimed, and many others, and cast them down at Jesus' feet; and he healed them:

31 Insomuch that the multitude wondered, when they saw the dumb to speak, the maimed to be whole, the lame to walk, and the blind to see: and they glorified the God of Israel.

—Matthew 15:30-31

And I will give unto thee the keys of the kingdom of heaven: and whatsoever thou shalt bind on earth shall be bound in heaven: and whatsoever thou shalt loose on earth shall be loosed in heaven.

—Matthew 16:19

[20] And Jesus said unto them, Because of your unbelief: for verily I say unto you, If ye have faith as a grain of mustard seed, ye shall say unto this mountain, Remove hence to yonder place; and it shall remove; and nothing shall be impossible unto you.

[21] Howbeit this kind goeth not out but by prayer and fasting.

—Matthew 17:20-21

[18] Verily I say unto you, Whatsoever ye shall bind on earth shall be bound in heaven: and whatsoever ye shall loose on earth shall be loosed in heaven.

[19] Again I say unto you, That if two of you shall agree on earth as touching any thing that they shall ask, it shall be done for them of my Father which is in heaven.

[20] For where two or three are gathered together in my name, there am I in the midst of them.

—Matthew 18:18-20

1 And it came to pass, that when Jesus had finished these sayings, he departed from Galilee, and came into the coasts of Judaea beyond Jordan;

[2] And great multitudes followed him; and he healed them there.

—Matthew 19:1-2

²⁹ And as they departed from Jericho, a great multitude followed him.

³⁰ And, behold, two blind men sitting by the way side, when they heard that Jesus passed by, cried out, saying, Have mercy on us, O Lord, thou son of David.

³¹ And the multitude rebuked them, because they should hold their peace: but they cried the more, saying, Have mercy on us, O Lord, thou son of David.

³² And Jesus stood still, and called them, and said, What will ye that I shall do unto you?

³³ They say unto him, Lord, that our eyes may be opened.

³⁴ So Jesus had compassion on them, and touched their eyes: and immediately their eyes received sight, and they followed him.

—Matthew 20:29-34

And the blind and the lame came to him in the temple; and he healed them.

—Matthew 21:14

²¹ Jesus answered and said unto them, Verily I say unto you, If ye have faith, and doubt not, ye shall not only do this which is done to the fig tree, but also if ye shall say unto this mountain, Be thou removed, and be thou cast into the sea; it shall be done.

²² And all things, whatsoever ye shall ask in prayer, believing, ye shall receive.

—Matthew 21:21-22

²⁹ And forthwith, when they were come out of the synagogue, they entered into the house of Simon and Andrew, with James and John.

30 But Simon's wife's mother lay sick of a fever, and anon they tell him of her.

31 And he came and took her by the hand, and lifted her up; and immediately the fever left her, and she ministered unto them.

32 And at even, when the sun did set, they brought unto him all that were diseased, and them that were possessed with devils.

33 And all the city was gathered together at the door.

34 And he healed many that were sick of divers diseases, and cast out many devils; and suffered not the devils to speak, because they knew him.

35 And in the morning, rising up a great while before day, he went out, and departed into a solitary place, and there prayed.

36 And Simon and they that were with him followed after him.

37 And when they had found him, they said unto him, All men seek for thee.

38 And he said unto them, Let us go into the next towns, that I may preach there also: for therefore came I forth.

39 And he preached in their synagogues throughout all Galilee, and cast out devils.

40 And there came a leper to him, beseeching him, and kneeling down to him, and saying unto him, If thou wilt, thou canst make me clean.

41 And Jesus, moved with compassion, put forth his hand, and touched him, and saith unto him, I will; be thou clean.

42 And as soon as he had spoken, immediately the leprosy departed from him, and he was cleansed.

—Mark 1:29-42

For he had healed many, so that those with diseases were pushing forward to touch him.
—Mark 3:10

And his fame went throughout all Syria: and they brought unto him all sick people that were taken with divers diseases and torments, and those which were possessed with devils, and those which were lunatick, and those that had the palsy; and he healed them.
—Mark 4:24

[18] And when he was come into the ship, he that had been possessed with the devil prayed him that he might be with him.

[19] Howbeit Jesus suffered him not, but saith unto him, Go home to thy friends, and tell them how great things the Lord hath done for thee, and hath had compassion on thee.

[20] And he departed, and began to publish in Decapolis how great things Jesus had done for him: and all men did marvel.
—Mark 5:18-20

[21] And when Jesus was passed over again by ship unto the other side, much people gathered unto him: and he was nigh unto the sea.

[22] And, behold, there cometh one of the rulers of the synagogue, Jairus by name; and when he saw him, he fell at his feet,

[23] And besought him greatly, saying, My little daughter lieth at the point of death: I pray thee, come and lay thy hands on her, that she may be healed; and she shall live.

HIS HEALING POWER

[24] And Jesus went with him; and much people followed him, and thronged him.

[25] And a certain woman, which had an issue of blood twelve years,

[26] And had suffered many things of many physicians, and had spent all that she had, and was nothing bettered, but rather grew worse,

[27] When she had heard of Jesus, came in the press behind, and touched his garment.

[28] For she said, If I may touch but his clothes, I shall be whole.

[29] And straightway the fountain of her blood was dried up; and she felt in her body that she was healed of that plague.

[30] And Jesus, immediately knowing in himself that virtue had gone out of him, turned him about in the press, and said, Who touched my clothes?

[31] And his disciples said unto him, Thou seest the multitude thronging thee, and sayest thou, Who touched me?

[32] And he looked round about to see her that had done this thing.

[33] But the woman fearing and trembling, knowing what was done in her, came and fell down before him, and told him all the truth.

[34] And he said unto her, Daughter, thy faith hath made thee whole; go in peace, and be whole of thy plague.

[35] While he yet spake, there came from the ruler of the synagogue's house certain which said, Thy daughter is dead: why troublest thou the Master any further?

[36] As soon as Jesus heard the word that was spoken, he saith unto the ruler of the synagogue, Be not afraid, only believe.

⁳⁷ And he suffered no man to follow him, save Peter, and James, and John the brother of James.

³⁸ And he cometh to the house of the ruler of the synagogue, and seeth the tumult, and them that wept and wailed greatly.

³⁹ And when he was come in, he saith unto them, Why make ye this ado, and weep? the damsel is not dead, but sleepeth.

⁴⁰ And they laughed him to scorn. But when he had put them all out, he taketh the father and the mother of the damsel, and them that were with him, and entereth in where the damsel was lying.

⁴¹ And he took the damsel by the hand, and said unto her, Talitha cumi; which is, being interpreted, Damsel, I say unto thee, arise.

⁴² And straightway the damsel arose, and walked; for she was of the age of twelve years. And they were astonished with a great astonishment.

⁴³ And he charged them straitly that no man should know it; and commanded that something should be given her to eat.

—Mark 5:21-43

⁵ And he could there do no mighty work, save that he laid his hands upon a few sick folk, and healed them.

⁶ And he marvelled because of their unbelief. And he went round about the villages, teaching.

⁷ And he called unto him the twelve, and began to send them forth by two and two; and gave them power over unclean spirits . . .

¹² And they went out, and preached that men should repent.

¹³ And they cast out many devils, and anointed with oil many that were sick, and healed them.

—Mark 6:5-7,12-13

⁵³ And when they had passed over, they came into the land of Gennesaret, and drew to the shore.

⁵⁴ And when they were come out of the ship, straightway they knew him,

⁵⁵ And ran through that whole region round about, and began to carry about in beds those that were sick, where they heard he was.

⁵⁶ And whithersoever he entered, into villages, or cities, or country, they laid the sick in the streets, and besought him that they might touch if it were but the border of his garment: and as many as touched him were made whole.

—Mark 6:53-56

31 And again, departing from the coasts of Tyre and Sidon, he came unto the sea of Galilee, through the midst of the coasts of Decapolis.

³² And they bring unto him one that was deaf, and had an impediment in his speech; and they beseech him to put his hand upon him.

³³ And he took him aside from the multitude, and put his fingers into his ears, and he spit, and touched his tongue;

³⁴ And looking up to heaven, he sighed, and saith unto him, Ephphatha, that is, Be opened.

³⁵ And straightway his ears were opened, and the string of his tongue was loosed, and he spake plain.

36 And he charged them that they should tell no man: but the more he charged them, so much the more a great deal they published it;

37 And were beyond measure astonished, saying, He hath done all things well: he maketh both the deaf to hear, and the dumb to speak.

—Mark 7:31-37

22 And he cometh to Bethsaida; and they bring a blind man unto him, and besought him to touch him.

23 And he took the blind man by the hand, and led him out of the town; and when he had spit on his eyes, and put his hands upon him, he asked him if he saw ought.

24 And he looked up, and said, I see men as trees, walking.

25 After that he put his hands again upon his eyes, and made him look up: and he was restored, and saw every man clearly.

—Mark 8:22-25

14 And when he came to his disciples, he saw a great multitude about them, and the scribes questioning with them.

15 And straightway all the people, when they beheld him, were greatly amazed, and running to him saluted him.

16 And he asked the scribes, What question ye with them?

17 And one of the multitude answered and said, Master, I have brought unto thee my son, which hath a dumb spirit;

18 And wheresoever he taketh him, he teareth him: and he foameth, and gnasheth with his teeth, and pineth

away: and I spake to thy disciples that they should cast him out; and they could not.

¹⁹ He answereth him, and saith, O faithless generation, how long shall I be with you? how long shall I suffer you? bring him unto me.

²⁰ And they brought him unto him: and when he saw him, straightway the spirit tare him; and he fell on the ground, and wallowed foaming.

²¹ And he asked his father, How long is it ago since this came unto him? And he said, Of a child.

²² And ofttimes it hath cast him into the fire, and into the waters, to destroy him: but if thou canst do any thing, have compassion on us, and help us.

²³ Jesus said unto him, If thou canst believe, all things are possible to him that believeth.

²⁴ And straightway the father of the child cried out, and said with tears, Lord, I believe; help thou mine unbelief.

²⁵ When Jesus saw that the people came running together, he rebuked the foul spirit, saying unto him, Thou dumb and deaf spirit, I charge thee, come out of him, and enter no more into him.

²⁶ And the spirit cried, and rent him sore, and came out of him: and he was as one dead; insomuch that many said, He is dead.

²⁷ But Jesus took him by the hand, and lifted him up; and he arose.

²⁸ And when he was come into the house, his disciples asked him privately, Why could not we cast him out?

²⁹ And he said unto them, This kind can come forth by nothing, but by prayer and fasting.

—Mark 9:14-29

⁴⁶ And they came to Jericho: and as he went out of Jericho with his disciples and a great number of people, blind Bartimaeus, the son of Timaeus, sat by the highway side begging.

⁴⁷ And when he heard that it was Jesus of Nazareth, he began to cry out, and say, Jesus, thou son of David, have mercy on me.

⁴⁸ And many charged him that he should hold his peace: but he cried the more a great deal, Thou son of David, have mercy on me.

⁴⁹ And Jesus stood still, and commanded him to be called. And they call the blind man, saying unto him, Be of good comfort, rise; he calleth thee.

⁵⁰ And he, casting away his garment, rose, and came to Jesus.

⁵¹ And Jesus answered and said unto him, What wilt thou that I should do unto thee? The blind man said unto him, Lord, that I might receive my sight.

⁵² And Jesus said unto him, Go thy way; thy faith hath made thee whole. And immediately he received his sight, and followed Jesus in the way.

—Mark 10:46-52

²² And Jesus answering saith unto them, Have faith in God.

²³ For verily I say unto you, That whosoever shall say unto this mountain, Be thou removed, and be thou cast into the sea; and shall not doubt in his heart, but shall believe that those things which he saith shall come to pass; he shall have whatsoever he saith.

²⁴ Therefore I say unto you, What things soever ye desire, when ye pray, believe that ye receive them, and ye shall have them.

—Mark 11:22-24

As I read these scriptures, it becomes apparent that Jesus said that in order to receive anything from Him, we must ask in faith believing that it will come to pass. There can be no doubt in our hearts. If we believe when we pray that we have received what we have asked for, we will have whatever we desire and ask of Him.

When He was in His hometown of Nazareth He marveled at their unbelief. They knew Him as the carpenter's son and not The Healer. He could not there heal those who refused to believe. Not wouldn't. Couldn't. Belief in Him that He will do what He says He will do and heal is the essential first step to receiving our healing.

In the areas where the people came running to Him, bringing the sick on mats for Him to heal them, He healed them all.

14 Afterward he appeared unto the eleven as they sat at meat, and upbraided them with their unbelief and hardness of heart, because they believed not them which had seen him after he was risen.

15 And he said unto them, Go ye into all the world, and preach the gospel to every creature.

16 He that believeth and is baptized shall be saved; but he that believeth not shall be damned.

17 And these signs shall follow them that believe; In my name shall they cast out devils; they shall speak with new tongues;

[18] They shall take up serpents; and if they drink any deadly thing, it shall not hurt them; they shall lay hands on the sick, and they shall recover.
—Mark 16:14-18

[14] And Jesus returned in the power of the Spirit into Galilee: and there went out a fame of him through all the region round about.

[15] And he taught in their synagogues, being glorified of all.

[16] And he came to Nazareth, where he had been brought up: and, as his custom was, he went into the synagogue on the sabbath day, and stood up for to read.

[17] And there was delivered unto him the book of the prophet Esaias. And when he had opened the book, he found the place where it was written,

[18] The Spirit of the Lord is upon me, because he hath anointed me to preach the gospel to the poor; he hath sent me to heal the brokenhearted, to preach deliverance to the captives, and recovering of sight to the blind, to set at liberty them that are bruised,

[19] To preach the acceptable year of the Lord.

[20] And he closed the book, and he gave it again to the minister, and sat down. And the eyes of all them that were in the synagogue were fastened on him.

[21] And he began to say unto them, This day is this scripture fulfilled in your ears.
—Luke 4:14-21

[38] And he arose out of the synagogue, and entered into Simon's house. And Simon's wife's mother was taken with a great fever; and they besought him for her.

HIS HEALING POWER

[39] And he stood over her, and rebuked the fever; and it left her: and immediately she arose and ministered unto them.

[40] Now when the sun was setting, all they that had any sick with divers diseases brought them unto him; and he laid his hands on every one of them, and healed them.

—Luke 4:38-40

[15] But so much the more went there a fame abroad of him: and great multitudes came together to hear, and to be healed by him of their infirmities.

[16] And he withdrew himself into the wilderness, and prayed.

[17] And it came to pass on a certain day, as he was teaching, that there were Pharisees and doctors of the law sitting by, which were come out of every town of Galilee, and Judaea, and Jerusalem: and the power of the Lord was present to heal them.

[18] And, behold, men brought in a bed a man which was taken with a palsy: and they sought means to bring him in, and to lay him before him.

[19] And when they could not find by what way they might bring him in because of the multitude, they went upon the housetop, and let him down through the tiling with his couch into the midst before Jesus.

[20] And when he saw their faith, he said unto him, Man, thy sins are forgiven thee.

[24] But that ye may know that the Son of man hath power upon earth to forgive sins, (he said unto the sick of the palsy,) I say unto thee, Arise, and take up thy couch, and go into thine house.

^{25} And immediately he rose up before them, and took up that whereon he lay, and departed to his own house, glorifying God.

—Luke 5:15-20, 24-25

^{17} And he came down with them, and stood in the plain, and the company of his disciples, and a great multitude of people out of all Judaea and Jerusalem, and from the sea coast of Tyre and Sidon, which came to hear him, and to be healed of their diseases;

^{18} And they that were vexed with unclean spirits: and they were healed.

^{19} And the whole multitude sought to touch him: for there went virtue out of him, and healed them all.

—Luke 6:17-19

^{11} And it came to pass the day after, that he went into a city called Nain; and many of his disciples went with him, and much people.

^{12} Now when he came nigh to the gate of the city, behold, there was a dead man carried out, the only son of his mother, and she was a widow: and much people of the city was with her.

^{13} And when the Lord saw her, he had compassion on her, and said unto her, Weep not.

^{14} And he came and touched the bier: and they that bare him stood still. And he said, Young man, I say unto thee, Arise.

^{15} And he that was dead sat up, and began to speak. And he delivered him to his mother.

—Luke 7:11-15

HIS HEALING POWER

⁴⁰ And it came to pass, that, when Jesus was returned, the people gladly received him: for they were all waiting for him.

⁴¹ And, behold, there came a man named Jairus, and he was a ruler of the synagogue: and he fell down at Jesus' feet, and besought him that he would come into his house:

⁴² For he had one only daughter, about twelve years of age, and she lay a dying. But as he went the people thronged him.

⁴³ And a woman having an issue of blood twelve years, which had spent all her living upon physicians, neither could be healed of any,

⁴⁴ Came behind him, and touched the border of his garment: and immediately her issue of blood stanched.

⁴⁵ And Jesus said, Who touched me? When all denied, Peter and they that were with him said, Master, the multitude throng thee and press thee, and sayest thou, Who touched me?

⁴⁶ And Jesus said, Somebody hath touched me: for I perceive that virtue is gone out of me.

⁴⁷ And when the woman saw that she was not hid, she came trembling, and falling down before him, she declared unto him before all the people for what cause she had touched him, and how she was healed immediately.

⁴⁸ And he said unto her, Daughter, be of good comfort: thy faith hath made thee whole; go in peace.

⁴⁹ While he yet spake, there cometh one from the ruler of the synagogue's house, saying to him, Thy daughter is dead; trouble not the Master.

⁵⁰ But when Jesus heard it, he answered him, saying, Fear not: believe only, and she shall be made whole.

⁵¹ And when he came into the house, he suffered no man to go in, save Peter, and James, and John, and the father and the mother of the maiden.

⁵² And all wept, and bewailed her: but he said, Weep not; she is not dead, but sleepeth.

⁵³ And they laughed him to scorn, knowing that she was dead.

⁵⁴ And he put them all out, and took her by the hand, and called, saying, Maid, arise.

⁵⁵ And her spirit came again, and she arose straightway: and he commanded to give her meat.

—Luke 8:40-55

¹ Then he called his twelve disciples together, and gave them power and authority over all devils, and to cure diseases.

² And he sent them to preach the kingdom of God, and to heal the sick. . . .

⁶ And they departed, and went through the towns, preaching the gospel, and healing every where. . . .

¹⁰ And the apostles, when they were returned, told him all that they had done. And he took them, and went aside privately into a desert place belonging to the city called Bethsaida.

¹¹ And the people, when they knew it, followed him: and he received them, and spake unto them of the kingdom of God, and healed them that had need of healing.

—Luke 9:1-2, 6, 10-11

¹ After these things the LORD appointed other seventy also, and sent them two and two before his face into every city and place, whither he himself would come.

² Therefore said he unto them, The harvest truly is great, but the labourers are few: pray ye therefore the Lord of the harvest, that he would send forth labourers into his harvest.

³ Go your ways: behold, I send you forth as lambs among wolves. . . .

⁸ And into whatsoever city ye enter, and they receive you, eat such things as are set before you:

⁹ And heal the sick that are therein, and say unto them, The kingdom of God is come nigh unto you.

—Luke 10:1-3, 8-9

¹⁰ And he was teaching in one of the synagogues on the sabbath.

¹¹ And, behold, there was a woman which had a spirit of infirmity eighteen years, and was bowed together, and could in no wise lift up herself.

¹² And when Jesus saw her, he called her to him, and said unto her, Woman, thou art loosed from thine infirmity.

¹³ And he laid his hands on her: and immediately she was made straight, and glorified God.

¹⁴ And the ruler of the synagogue answered with indignation, because that Jesus had healed on the sabbath day, and said unto the people, There are six days in which men ought to work: in them therefore come and be healed, and not on the sabbath day.

¹⁵ The Lord then answered him, and said, Thou hypocrite, doth not each one of you on the sabbath loose his ox or his ass from the stall, and lead him away to watering?

¹⁶ And ought not this woman, being a daughter of Abraham, whom Satan hath bound, lo, these eighteen years, be loosed from this bond on the sabbath day?

¹⁷ And when he had said these things, all his adversaries were ashamed: and all the people rejoiced for all the glorious things that were done by him.

—Luke 13:10-17

² And, behold, there was a certain man before him which had the dropsy.

³ And Jesus answering spake unto the lawyers and Pharisees, saying, Is it lawful to heal on the sabbath day?

⁴ And they held their peace. And he took him, and healed him, and let him go;

—Luke 14:2-4

¹¹ And it came to pass, as he went to Jerusalem, that he passed through the midst of Samaria and Galilee.

¹² And as he entered into a certain village, there met him ten men that were lepers, which stood afar off:

¹³ And they lifted up their voices, and said, Jesus, Master, have mercy on us.

¹⁴ And when he saw them, he said unto them, Go shew yourselves unto the priests. And it came to pass, that, as they went, they were cleansed.

¹⁵ And one of them, when he saw that he was healed, turned back, and with a loud voice glorified God,

¹⁶ And fell down on his face at his feet, giving him thanks: and he was a Samaritan.

¹⁷ And Jesus answering said, Were there not ten cleansed? but where are the nine?

¹⁸ There are not found that returned to give glory to God, save this stranger.

¹⁹ And he said unto him, Arise, go thy way: thy faith hath made thee whole.

—Luke 17:11-19

The very first thing the woman who was bowed over with the spirit of infirmity did when Jesus healed her was to glorify and praise God for her healing. Jesus healed 10 lepers but only one returned to glorify and praise God. Jesus healed all 10 of them from leprosy. To the one who returned to glorify God, He said, "Thy faith hath made thee whole." Not only his body but also his whole life was restored to wholeness, because he chose to return and praise and thank God for his healing.

So glorifying and praising and thanking God should be the first thing we do when we are healed. Actually we should be in obedience to what Jesus told us to do in Mark 11:24, (What things soever ye desire, when ye pray, believe that ye receive them, and ye shall have them.) If we have healing when we pray for it, we should begin immediately to thank and praise God for it. Jesus told us to believe in our hearts and not doubt or waver. (But let him ask in faith, nothing wavering. For he that wavereth is like a wave of the sea driven with the wind and tossed. James 1:6) So if we receive what we ask when we pray for it in faith believing, all that's left to do is praise and glorify God. (Let us hold fast the

profession of our faith without wavering; for he is faithful that promised. Hebrews 10:23)

^{47} And while he yet spake, behold a multitude, and he that was called Judas, one of the twelve, went before them, and drew near unto Jesus to kiss him.

^{48} But Jesus said unto him, Judas, betrayest thou the Son of man with a kiss?

^{49} When they which were about him saw what would follow, they said unto him, Lord, shall we smite with the sword?

^{50} And one of them smote the servant of the high priest, and cut off his right ear.

^{51} And Jesus answered and said, Suffer ye thus far. And he touched his ear, and healed him.

—Luke 22:47-51

^{46} So Jesus came again into Cana of Galilee, where he made the water wine. And there was a certain nobleman, whose son was sick at Capernaum.

^{47} When he heard that Jesus was come out of Judaea into Galilee, he went unto him, and besought him that he would come down, and heal his son: for he was at the point of death.

^{48} Then said Jesus unto him, Except ye see signs and wonders, ye will not believe.

^{49} The nobleman saith unto him, Sir, come down ere my child die.

^{50} Jesus saith unto him, Go thy way; thy son liveth. And the man believed the word that Jesus had spoken unto him, and he went his way.

⁵¹ And as he was now going down, his servants met him, and told him, saying, Thy son liveth.

⁵² Then enquired he of them the hour when he began to amend. And they said unto him, Yesterday at the seventh hour the fever left him.

⁵³ So the father knew that it was at the same hour, in which Jesus said unto him, Thy son liveth: and himself believed, and his whole house.

—John 4:46-53

¹ After this there was a feast of the Jews; and Jesus went up to Jerusalem.

² Now there is at Jerusalem by the sheep market a pool, which is called in the Hebrew tongue Bethesda, having five porches.

³ In these lay a great multitude of impotent folk, of blind, halt, withered, waiting for the moving of the water.

⁴ For an angel went down at a certain season into the pool, and troubled the water: whosoever then first after the troubling of the water stepped in was made whole of whatsoever disease he had.

⁵ And a certain man was there, which had an infirmity thirty and eight years.

⁶ When Jesus saw him lie, and knew that he had been now a long time in that case, he saith unto him, Wilt thou be made whole?

⁷ The impotent man answered him, Sir, I have no man, when the water is troubled, to put me into the pool: but while I am coming, another steppeth down before me.

⁸ Jesus saith unto him, Rise, take up thy bed, and walk.

⁹ And immediately the man was made whole, and took up his bed, and walked: and on the same day was the sabbath.

—John 5:1-9

The thief cometh not, but for to steal, and to kill, and to destroy: I am come that they might have life, and that they might have it more abundantly.

—John 10:10

When Jesus heard that, he said, This sickness is not unto death, but for the glory of God, that the Son of God might be glorified thereby.

—John 11:4

¹² Verily, verily, I say unto you, He that believeth on me, the works that I do shall he do also; and greater works than these shall he do; because I go unto my Father.

¹³ And whatsoever ye shall ask in my name, that will I do, that the Father may be glorified in the Son.

¹⁴ If ye shall ask any thing in my name, I will do it.

—John 14:12-14

Peace I leave with you, my peace I give unto you: not as the world giveth, give I unto you. Let not your heart be troubled, neither let it be afraid.

—John 14:27

If ye abide in me, and my words abide in you, ye shall ask what ye will, and it shall be done unto you.

—John 15:7

²³ And in that day ye shall ask me nothing. Verily, verily, I say unto you, Whatsoever ye shall ask the Father in my name, he will give it you.

HIS HEALING POWER

^{24} Hitherto have ye asked nothing in my name: ask, and ye shall receive, that your joy may be full.

—John 16:23-24

^{1} Now Peter and John went up together into the temple at the hour of prayer, being the ninth hour.

^{2} And a certain man lame from his mother's womb was carried, whom they laid daily at the gate of the temple which is called Beautiful, to ask alms of them that entered into the temple;

^{3} Who seeing Peter and John about to go into the temple asked an alms.

^{4} And Peter, fastening his eyes upon him with John, said, Look on us.

^{5} And he gave heed unto them, expecting to receive something of them.

^{6} Then Peter said, Silver and gold have I none; but such as I have give I thee: In the name of Jesus Christ of Nazareth rise up and walk.

^{7} And he took him by the right hand, and lifted him up: and immediately his feet and ankle bones received strength.

^{8} And he leaping up stood, and walked, and entered with them into the temple, walking, and leaping, and praising God.

^{9} And all the people saw him walking and praising God:

^{10} And they knew that it was he which sat for alms at the Beautiful gate of the temple: and they were filled with wonder and amazement at that which had happened unto him. . . .

^{16} And his name through faith in his name hath made this man strong, whom ye see and know: yea,

the faith which is by him hath given him this perfect soundness in the presence of you all.
—Acts 3:1-10, 16

¹² And by the hands of the apostles were many signs and wonders wrought among the people; (and they were all with one accord in Solomon's porch.

¹³ And of the rest durst no man join himself to them: but the people magnified them.

¹⁴ And believers were the more added to the Lord, multitudes both of men and women.)

¹⁵ Insomuch that they brought forth the sick into the streets, and laid them on beds and couches, that at the least the shadow of Peter passing by might overshadow some of them.

¹⁶ There came also a multitude out of the cities round about unto Jerusalem, bringing sick folks, and them which were vexed with unclean spirits: and they were healed every one.
—Acts 5:12-16

⁵ Then Philip went down to the city of Samaria, and preached Christ unto them.

⁶ And the people with one accord gave heed unto those things which Philip spake, hearing and seeing the miracles which he did.

⁷ For unclean spirits, crying with loud voice, came out of many that were possessed with them: and many taken with palsies, and that were lame, were healed.

⁸ And there was great joy in that city.
—Acts 8:5-8

HIS HEALING POWER

³² And it came to pass, as Peter passed throughout all quarters, he came down also to the saints which dwelt at Lydda.

³³ And there he found a certain man named Aeneas, which had kept his bed eight years, and was sick of the palsy.

³⁴ And Peter said unto him, Aeneas, Jesus Christ maketh thee whole: arise, and make thy bed. And he arose immediately.

³⁵ And all that dwelt at Lydda and Saron saw him, and turned to the Lord.

—Acts 9:32-35

How God anointed Jesus of Nazareth with the Holy Ghost and with power: who went about doing good, and healing all that were oppressed of the devil; for God was with him.

—Acts 10:38

⁸ And there sat a certain man at Lystra, impotent in his feet, being a cripple from his mother's womb, who never had walked:

⁹ The same heard Paul speak: who stedfastly beholding him, and perceiving that he had faith to be healed,

¹⁰ Said with a loud voice, Stand upright on thy feet. And he leaped and walked.

—Acts 14:8-10

¹ God that made the world and all things therein, seeing that he is Lord of heaven and earth, dwelleth not in temples made with hands;

²⁵ Neither is worshipped with men's hands, as though he needed any thing, seeing he giveth to all life, and breath, and all things;

—Acts 17:24-25

¹¹ And God wrought special miracles by the hands of Paul:

¹² So that from his body were brought unto the sick handkerchiefs or aprons, and the diseases departed from them, and the evil spirits went out of them.

—Acts 19:11-12

¹ And when they were escaped, then they knew that the island was called Melita.

² And the barbarous people shewed us no little kindness: for they kindled a fire, and received us every one, because of the present rain, and because of the cold.

³ And when Paul had gathered a bundle of sticks, and laid them on the fire, there came a viper out of the heat, and fastened on his hand.

⁴ And when the barbarians saw the venomous beast hang on his hand, they said among themselves, No doubt this man is a murderer, whom, though he hath escaped the sea, yet vengeance suffereth not to live.

⁵ And he shook off the beast into the fire, and felt no harm.

⁶ Howbeit they looked when he should have swollen, or fallen down dead suddenly: but after they had looked a great while, and saw no harm come to him, they changed their minds, and said that he was a god.

⁷ In the same quarters were possessions of the chief man of the island, whose name was Publius; who received us, and lodged us three days courteously.

8 And it came to pass, that the father of Publius lay sick of a fever and of a bloody flux: to whom Paul entered in, and prayed, and laid his hands on him, and healed him.

HIS HEALING POWER

9 So when this was done, others also, which had diseases in the island, came, and were healed:

—Acts 28:1-9

16 For I am not ashamed of the gospel of Christ: for it is the power of God unto salvation to every one that believeth; to the Jew first, and also to the Greek.

17 For therein is the righteousness of God revealed from faith to faith: as it is written, The just shall live by faith.

—Romans 1:16-17

16 Therefore it is of faith, that it might be by grace; to the end the promise might be sure to all the seed; not to that only which is of the law, but to that also which is of the faith of Abraham; who is the father of us all,

17 (As it is written, I have made thee a father of many nations,) before him whom he believed, even God, who quickeneth the dead, and calleth those things which be not as though they were.

18 Who against hope believed in hope, that he might become the father of many nations, according to that which was spoken, So shall thy seed be.

19 And being not weak in faith, he considered not his own body now dead, when he was about an hundred years old, neither yet the deadness of Sarah's womb:

20 He staggered not at the promise of God through unbelief; but was strong in faith, giving glory to God;

21 And being fully persuaded that, what he had promised, he was able also to perform.

—Romans 4:16-21

But what saith it? The word is nigh thee, even in thy mouth, and in thy heart: that is, the word of faith, which we preach;

—Romans 10:8

So then faith cometh by hearing, and hearing by the word of God.

—Romans 10:17

[1] I beseech you therefore, brethren, by the mercies of God, that ye present your bodies a living sacrifice, holy, acceptable unto God, which is your reasonable service.

[2] And be not conformed to this world: but be ye transformed by the renewing of your mind, that ye may prove what is that good, and acceptable, and perfect, will of God.

—Romans 12:1-2

[19] What? know ye not that your body is the temple of the Holy Ghost which is in you, which ye have of God, and ye are not your own?

[20] For ye are bought with a price: therefore glorify God in your body, and in your spirit, which are God's.

—1 Corinthians 6:19-20

[23] For I have received of the Lord that which also I delivered unto you, that the Lord Jesus the same night in which he was betrayed took bread:

[24] And when he had given thanks, he brake it, and said, Take, eat: this is my body, which is broken for you: this do in remembrance of me.

²⁵ After the same manner also he took the cup, when he had supped, saying, this cup is the new testament in my blood: this do ye, as oft as ye drink it, in remembrance of me.

²⁶ For as often as ye eat this bread, and drink this cup, ye do shew the Lord's death till he come.

²⁷ Wherefore whosoever shall eat this bread, and drink this cup of the Lord, unworthily, shall be guilty of the body and blood of the Lord.

²⁸ But let a man examine himself, and so let him eat of that bread, and drink of that cup.

²⁹ For he that eateth and drinketh unworthily, eateth and drinketh damnation to himself, not discerning the Lord's body.

³⁰ For this cause many are weak and sickly among you, and many sleep.

³¹ For if we would judge ourselves, we should not be judged.

³² But when we are judged, we are chastened of the Lord, that we should not be condemned with the world.

—1 Corinthians 11:23-32

For God is not the author of confusion, but of peace, as in all churches of the saints.

—1 Corinthians 14:33

³ Grace be unto you, and peace, from God our Father, and from the Lord Jesus Christ.

⁴ I thank my God always on your behalf, for the grace of God which is given you by Jesus Christ;

⁵ That in every thing ye are enriched by him, in all utterance, and in all knowledge;

—1 Corinthians 1:3-5

For we walk by faith, not by sight.

—2 Corinthians 5:7

We believe what the WORD of God says about our situation, not what our eyes tell us. That's what faith is.

³ For though we walk in the flesh, we do not war after the flesh:

⁴ (For the weapons of our warfare are not carnal, but mighty through God to the pulling down of strong holds;)

⁵ Casting down imaginations, and every high thing that exalteth itself against the knowledge of God, and bringing into captivity every thought to the obedience of Christ.

—2 Corinthians 10:3-5

And he said unto me, My grace is sufficient for thee: for my strength is made perfect in weakness. Most gladly therefore will I rather glory in my infirmities, that the power of Christ may rest upon me.

—2 Corinthians 12:9

¹ Children, obey your parents in the Lord: for this is right.

² Honour thy father and mother; which is the first commandment with promise;

³ That it may be well with thee, and thou mayest live long on the earth.

—Ephesians 6:1-3

10 Finally, my brethren, be strong in the Lord, and in the power of his might.

¹¹ Put on the whole armour of God, that ye may be able to stand against the wiles of the devil.

¹² For we wrestle not against flesh and blood, but against principalities, against powers, against the rulers of the darkness of this world, against spiritual wickedness in high places.

¹³ Wherefore take unto you the whole armour of God, that ye may be able to withstand in the evil day, and having done all, to stand.

¹⁴ Stand therefore, having your loins girt about with truth, and having on the breastplate of righteousness;

¹⁵ And your feet shod with the preparation of the gospel of peace;

¹⁶ Above all, taking the shield of faith, wherewith ye shall be able to quench all the fiery darts of the wicked.

¹⁷ And take the helmet of salvation, and the sword of the Spirit, which is the word of God:

¹⁸ Praying always with all prayer and supplication in the Spirit, and watching thereunto with all perseverance and supplication for all saints;

—Ephesians 6:10-18

Jesus said the enemy comes to steal, kill, and destroy. Sickness and disease are of and from the enemy. Jesus bore all our sicknesses and diseases on the cross so we don't have to. That's not our job. He already did that for us to deliver us from the curse. (Christ hath redeemed us from the curse of the law, being made a curse for us: for it is written, Cursed is everyone that hangeth on a tree. Galatians 3:13) When we receive Jesus as our Lord and

NEW TESTAMENT

Savior and believe He came to this earth as God's only Son, died on the cross for us, and took all our sins, sicknesses, and diseases, by the stripes on His back we are healed, delivered, and set free from them! WE ARE HEALED! NOW! It's done! We are healed and delivered from all sin, sickness, disease, pains, griefs, and sorrows.

We must stand in faith believing that it is done. God has given us weapons of spiritual warfare. We need to don our spiritual armor and having done all, to just stand. Stand in faith believing we have already been delivered from sickness and disease. Stand in faith believing and praising God for sending His only Son to die on the cross and take all our sins, sicknesses, diseases, pains, griefs, and sorrows so we can go free. Healed and delivered.

[9] Wherefore God also hath highly exalted him, and given him a name which is above every name:

[10] That at the name of Jesus every knee should bow, of things in heaven, and things in earth, and things under the earth;

[11] And that every tongue should confess that Jesus Christ is Lord, to the glory of God the Father.

—Philippians 2:9-11

For it is God which worketh in you both to will and to do of his good pleasure.

—Philippians 2:13

[4] Rejoice in the Lord always: and again I say, Rejoice.

[5] Let your moderation be known unto all men. The Lord is at hand.

[6] Be careful for nothing; but in every thing by prayer and supplication with thanksgiving let your requests be made known unto God.

[7] And the peace of God, which passeth all understanding, shall keep your hearts and minds through Christ Jesus.

[8] Finally, brethren, whatsoever things are true, whatsoever things are honest, whatsoever things are just, whatsoever things are pure, whatsoever things are lovely, whatsoever things are of good report; if there be any virtue, and if there be any praise, think on these things.

[9] Those things, which ye have both learned, and received, and heard, and seen in me, do: and the God of peace shall be with you.

—Philippians 4:4-9

[19] But my God shall supply all your need according to his riches in glory by Christ Jesus.

[20] Now unto God and our Father be glory for ever and ever. Amen.

—Philippians 4:19-20

[13] Who hath delivered us from the power of darkness, and hath translated us into the kingdom of his dear Son:

[14] In whom we have redemption through his blood, even the forgiveness of sins:

—Colossians 1:13-14

And ye are complete in him, which is the head of all principality and power:
—Colossians 2:10

[13] And you, being dead in your sins and the uncircumcision of your flesh, hath he quickened together with him, having forgiven you all trespasses;

[14] Blotting out the handwriting of ordinances that was against us, which was contrary to us, and took it out of the way, nailing it to his cross;

[15] And having spoiled principalities and powers, he made a shew of them openly, triumphing over them in it.
—Colossians 2:13-15

[23] And the very God of peace sanctify you wholly; and I pray God your whole spirit and soul and body be preserved blameless unto the coming of our Lord Jesus Christ.

[24] Faithful is he that calleth you, who also will do it.
—1 Thessalonians 5:23-24

For God hath not given us the spirit of fear; but of power, and of love, and of a sound mind.
—2 Timothy 1:7

[14] Seeing then that we have a great high priest, that is passed into the heavens, Jesus the Son of God, let us hold fast our profession.

[15] For we have not an high priest which cannot be touched with the feeling of our infirmities; but was in all points tempted like as we are, yet without sin.

¹⁶ Let us therefore come boldly unto the throne of grace, that we may obtain mercy, and find grace to help in time of need.

—Hebrews 4:14-16

¹¹ And we desire that every one of you do shew the same diligence to the full assurance of hope unto the end:

¹² That ye be not slothful, but followers of them who through faith and patience inherit the promises.

—Hebrews 6:11-12

As we stand in faith believing for healing to manifest in our bodies, patience is required. God has promised in His WORD that by His stripes we are healed. God is not a man that He should lie. His WORD is Truth. We stand in faith believing patiently until healing comes and physically manifests in our bodies. We stand in faith patiently praising God and resisting the enemy so he doesn't steal our healing. (Submit yourselves therefore to God. Resist the devil and he will flee from you. James 4:7)

¹⁶ For men verily swear by the greater: and an oath for confirmation is to them an end of all strife.

¹⁷ Wherein God, willing more abundantly to shew unto the heirs of promise the immutability of his counsel, confirmed it by an oath:

¹⁸ That by two immutable things, in which it was impossible for God to lie, we might have a strong

consolation, who have fled for refuge to lay hold upon the hope set before us:

¹⁹ Which hope we have as an anchor of the soul, both sure and stedfast, and which entereth into that within the veil;

²⁰ Whither the forerunner is for us entered, even Jesus, made an high priest for ever after the order of Melchisedec.
—Hebrews 6:16-20

²⁴ But this man, because he continueth ever, hath an unchangeable priesthood.

²⁵ Wherefore he is able also to save them to the uttermost that come unto God by him, seeing he ever liveth to make intercession for them.
—Hebrews 7:24-25

Let us hold fast the profession of our faith without wavering; (for he is faithful that promised;)
—Hebrews 10:23

³⁵ Cast not away therefore your confidence, which hath great recompence of reward.

³⁶ For ye have need of patience, that, after ye have done the will of God, ye might receive the promise.
—Hebrews 10:35-36

Now faith is the substance of things hoped for, the evidence of things not seen.
—Hebrews 11:1

Through faith also Sara herself received strength to conceive seed, and was delivered of a child when she was past age, because she judged him faithful who had promised.

—Hebrews 11:11

And make straight paths for your feet, lest that which is lame be turned out of the way; but let it rather be healed.

—Hebrews 12:13

Jesus Christ the same yesterday, and today, and forever.

—Hebrews 13:8

² For in many things we offend all. If any man offend not in word, the same is a perfect man, and able also to bridle the whole body.

³ Behold, we put bits in the horses' mouths, that they may obey us; and we turn about their whole body.

⁴ Behold also the ships, which though they be so great, and are driven of fierce winds, yet are they turned about with a very small helm, whithersoever the governor listeth.

⁵ Even so the tongue is a little member, and boasteth great things. Behold, how great a matter a little fire kindleth!

⁶ And the tongue is a fire, a world of iniquity: so is the tongue among our members, that it defileth the whole body, and setteth on fire the course of nature; and it is set on fire of hell.

—James 3:2-6

Submit yourselves therefore to God. Resist the devil, and he will flee from you.

—James 4:7

Behold, we count them happy which endure. Ye have heard of the patience of Job, and have seen the end of the Lord; that the Lord is very pitiful, and of tender mercy.

—James 5:11

¹³ Is any among you afflicted? let him pray. Is any merry? let him sing psalms.

¹⁴ Is any sick among you? let him call for the elders of the church; and let them pray over him, anointing him with oil in the name of the Lord:

¹⁵ And the prayer of faith shall save the sick, and the Lord shall raise him up; and if he have committed sins, they shall be forgiven him.

¹⁶ Confess your faults one to another, and pray one for another, that ye may be healed. The effectual fervent prayer of a righteous man availeth much.

—James 5:13-16

Who his own self bare our sins in his own body on the tree, that we, being dead to sins, should live unto righteousness: by whose stripes ye were healed.

—1 Peter 2:24

This is the key verse that sums up God's promise that we are healed by the stripes on Jesus' back on the cross. If we were healed, we are healed.

⁶ Humble yourselves therefore under the mighty hand of God, that he may exalt you in due time:

⁷ Casting all your care upon him; for he careth for you.

⁸ Be sober, be vigilant; because your adversary the devil, as a roaring lion, walketh about, seeking whom he may devour:

⁹ Whom resist stedfast in the faith, knowing that the same afflictions are accomplished in your brethren that are in the world.

¹⁰ But the God of all grace, who hath called us unto his eternal glory by Christ Jesus, after that ye have suffered a while, make you perfect, stablish, strengthen, settle you.

¹¹ To him be glory and dominion for ever and ever. Amen.

—1 Peter 5:6-11

² Grace and peace be multiplied unto you through the knowledge of God, and of Jesus our Lord,

³ According as his divine power hath given unto us all things that pertain unto life and godliness, through the knowledge of him that hath called us to glory and virtue:

⁴ Whereby are given unto us exceeding great and precious promises: that by these ye might be partakers of the divine nature, having escaped the corruption that is in the world through lust.

—2 Peter 1:2-4

²¹ Beloved, if our heart condemn us not, then have we confidence toward God.

²² And whatsoever we ask, we receive of him, because we keep his commandments, and do those things that are pleasing in his sight.

—1 John 3:21-22

Confession of faith: Greater is He that's within me than he that is in the world. (1 John 4:4) The Greater One lives within me and no sickness or disease can stand in His presence.

There is no fear in love; but perfect love casteth out fear: because fear hath torment. He that feareth is not made perfect in love.

—1 John 4:18

[14] And this is the confidence that we have in him, that, if we ask any thing according to his will, he heareth us:

[15] And if we know that he hear us, whatsoever we ask, we know that we have the petitions that we desired of him.

—1 John 5:14-15

Beloved, I wish above all things that thou mayest prosper and be in health, even as thy soul prospereth.

—3 John 2

God promises us over and over in His WORD that when we ask Him for anything according to His will He hears us. Healing is God's will for us. He also tells us this over and over in His WORD. If we know He hears us, we know we have the petitions we have asked of Him. We need only to stand in faith, believing patiently that we have what we ask, that it is done for us by our Father who is in Heaven. As we wait, we praise Him that it is already done. In Jesus' NAME! Amen.

And they overcame him by the blood of the Lamb, and by the word of their testimony; and they loved not their lives unto the death.
—Revelation 12:11

And God shall wipe away all tears from their eyes; and there shall be no more death, neither sorrow, nor crying, neither shall there be any more pain: for the former things are passed away.
—Revelation 21:4

NEW TESTAMENT

For God so loved the world, that He gave His only begotten Son, that whosoever believeth in Him should not perish, but have everlasting life.
—John 3:16

www.ingramcontent.com/pod-product-compliance
Lightning Source LLC
Chambersburg PA
CBHW042131080426
42735CB00005B/146